**PEARSON
PUBLISHING**

GW00702449

Victorian Britain

Stewart Ross

Illustrations by Julie Beer

ISBN 1 85749 091 6

Published by Pearson Publishing, Chesterton Mill, French's Road, Cambridge CB4 3NP

First edition 1993

Second edition 1995

Reprinted 1997

Text © Stewart Ross 1993

No part of this publication may be copied or reproduced, stored in a retrieval system or transmitted in any form or by any means electronic, mechanical, photocopy, recording or otherwise without the prior permission of the publisher.

Contents

Who were the Victorians?

The Queen

The word **Victorian** comes from a queen, named Victoria.

She was Queen of Great Britain from 1837 to 1901 – sixty-four years! Because she reigned for such a long time, and because many people became quite fond of her, her reign is known as the Victorian **era**.

Today we use the word Victorian to describe anything from that era, such as furniture, houses and books – even ideas and behaviour.

Queen Victoria, who gave her name to the Victorian era

Good times...

Many people think that in some ways life was better in Victorian times.

The sort of things they mean are:
- Britain was one of the most powerful countries in the world
- Many people seemed to behave better and know right from wrong
- People seemed more free, because the government did not **interfere** in their lives so much.

3

...or bad?

Historians say that life in Victorian Britain was not better or worse than today, just different. They point out that:

- It was often a cruel time – for example, most children were beaten by parents and teachers if they did something wrong.
- Women were not treated equally with men. For example, when they got married all their money became their husbands'.
- There was much more illness and poverty than today.

Children working in a factory in Victorian times

Class

People can be arranged into classes according to such things as their job, their education, what they do in their spare time and how much money they have.

The Victorians were much more interested in class than we are. They liked to place everyone in one of three classes:

- The upper class
- The middle class
- The working class

Most people were working class. Members of the upper and middle classes were often rather snobbish about them.

Problems with class

- Class is difficult to understand. Victorian people did not walk around wearing labels saying what class they belonged to!
- No one explained the meaning of each class exactly.
- It was not always clear which class a person belonged to.
- People's class was not fixed. If, for example, a middle-class family got rich enough to live without ever going to work, in time they would move from the middle class to the upper class.

What can you remember?

1   Fill in the gaps in these sentences with the right words from the following list:

   working class   reigned

   a   Queen Victoria _____ from 1837 to 1901.

   b   Most Victorians belonged to the _____.

2   What were the three classes which Victorians belonged to?

_____

Something to do

Colour the picture of Queen Victoria on page 3 and find out what relation Queen Elizabeth II is to Queen Victoria. _____

The Upper Class

Who was upper class?

The Victorian upper class was very small – about 3000 families. That may sound a lot, but it was only about one family in every 400!

Upper-class people were also very rich. This will give you some idea how rich:
- Working-class wages – between £25 and £100 a year.
- Income of the Duke of Bedford, an upper-class lord – more than £300 000 a year.

Men like the Duke of Bedford did not go out to work to earn their money. Their income came from the things they owned, such as land, mines and factories.

Waddesdon Manor, the stately home of upper-class Baron Rothschild

Aristocrats

At the very top of the upper class were the **aristocrats**, a handful of very wealthy lords and their families.

They all had at least two houses, one in London and one in the country. Most of them owned vast estates – most of England was owned by a very few families.

How did the aristocrats look after all their land and houses?

They certainly did not do the work themselves. Some of it was done by servants – the Duke of Westminster had 40 gardeners for just one of his houses! And some parts of their estates were let out for rent.

Gentry

Most of the upper class were not aristocrats, but **gentry**. They had an income of at least £1000 a year.

The gentry filled most of the important positions in the country – in the government, the army and navy, and the Church of England. Many of them knew each other. They went to the same schools and enjoyed the same hobbies and sports.

A dinner party for the gentry, 1882

The Middle Class

Change

The Britain of 1900 was very different from the Britain of 1830.

Two of the biggest changes were
1   the **population** had grown
2   the country was wealthier.

Because of these two changes, the middle class was larger and more important at the end of Victoria's reign than it had been at the beginning.

A middle-class Victorian family

Respectable people

By 1900 about one family in five was middle class, and the numbers were growing.

Some earned as much as £1000 a year, others as little as £50. But they did not do **manual work**, they had one or more servants and, above all, they tried to live respectable lives. They always wanted to behave and speak correctly, so they would not be mistaken for working-class people.

The picture at the bottom of page 7 shows an ideal Victorian middle-class family. They are clean, tidy, and well-dressed; the children are well-behaved; the mother is gentle and loving; the strong, kind father is looking after them all! Do you think many families were really like that?

The Working Class

All sorts and kinds

At least three-quarters of the population of Victorian Britain were working class. They might have been **skilled labourers**, earning as much as some middle-class families; or farm labourers; or badly paid factory workers; or poor people with no work and no money.

The type of house where some working-class families lived

City slums

In 1837 more people lived in the country than in towns. By 1901 there were three times as many people living in towns as in the country.

Thousands of houses were built to give cheap housing for town workers. They were often not well made. Many did not have lavatories or even running water. Water had to be brought in from an outside pump or tap.

Soon these badly-built houses started to fall to bits. The walls cracked, the roofs leaked, and rats and mice came to live there.

The picture on page 8 shows you what these houses were like. They were known as **slums**.

Overcrowding

As well as being horrible to live in, many working-class town houses were badly overcrowded. It was quite common for two families to share the same house. And some families had only one room to live in!

To make matters worse, families were much larger than today – imagine what it was like to have a mother and father and five or six children all sharing the same room, with no lavatory, no water, no kitchen and no bathroom.

Collecting water – can you see the wooden buckets?

1 The Victorians

By 1900 working-class life in the towns was usually better than it had been in the country. Even so, life for working-class people was very tough compared with the way the other two classes lived.

What can you remember?

Fill in the gaps in these sentences with the right words from the following list:

aristocracy   gentry   running water   manual work   population

1 The _____ of Britain grew enormously in Victorian times.

2 The upper class was made up of the _____ and the
_____.

3 The middle class did not do _____.

4 There was no _____ in the houses of many of the poor.

Something to do

1 Look carefully at this picture of a Victorian house and answer the questions below:

a Colour the picture and say which class of family you think lived there.

_____

b What are the reasons for the answer you gave?

_____

2 Find pictures of the clothes people wore in Victorian times. On a separate piece of paper, draw men and women, showing the different types of clothes they wore.

Steam

Measuring time

As you probably know, we measure the time each day in seconds, minutes and hours. 24 hours make a day. 365 days make a year. We call 100 years a **century**.

The first (1st) century after the birth of Jesus Christ we call the first century **AD**. It went from the year 1 AD to the year 100 AD. The 2nd century went from 101 AD to 200 AD. Normally we do not write the AD. The Victorian era was mostly in the 19th century (1801–1900).

Something to do

1   If there are 365 days in a year, how many days are there in a century?
_____

2   When did the tenth century begin and end? _____ to _____

3   What century are we in now? _____

Horses, wind and water

Until the 18th century there were no engines. The strongest power came from horses, the wind and water flowing in rivers and streams. The quickest way of travelling was by riding a horse or sailing in a ship. All ships were driven by sails. Heavy loads went in carts or in ships.

Large machines, like windmills and water mills, were powered by water or the wind. Small machines, like **spinning wheels** and **looms** were powered by people.

A spinning wheel

Steam engines

In the 18th century steam engines were invented. At first they were used just for pumping water. Then engines were made for working machines, like spinning machines and looms.

A little later, just before Victoria became queen, steam engines were fitted with wheels and put on metal lines – and so modern railways began. In this way the steam engine caused a **revolution** in the way things were made and transported.

A Victorian steam engine being used for ploughing, 1857

Still more power

By the end of the 19th century, steam was not the only new type of power. There were electric motors and petrol engines, used in cars. People could travel faster, carry heavier loads and make more in factories than ever before. Windmills, water mills and horses had become rather old-fashioned!

What can you remember?

1 What is a century? _____

2 In which century was the Victorian era? _____

3 What two new types of power were invented by 1900? _____ and
    _____

4 What were steam engines first used for? _____

Industry and Factories

Industrial revolution

Industry means making (or **manufacturing**) things. The industrial revolution was a complete change in the way most things were made. It began before Victoria became queen. Before that goods were made in small workshops or at home.

The industrial revolution meant goods could be made quickly and cheaply in large quantities, using factory machinery. The industrial revolution began in Britain and spread to other countries. In some places it is still happening.

Inside a Victorian factory

Coal

Coal powered the industrial revolution. It drove steam engines and was used for making iron, steel and bricks, and for heating. Huge clouds of smoke hung over Victorian cities.

Coal mining was a very dangerous job and not very well paid. When Victoria became queen, children worked in mines, pulling trucks down long, dark tunnels.

Iron

Before the industrial revolution, iron was made in charcoal fires. This was slow and used up many trees.

In the 18th century the **blast furnace** was invented, which allowed coke to be used for making iron. Now iron could be made quickly and in huge amounts.

2 Power

The iron bridge at Coalbrookdale,
built in 1779 to show what could be done with iron

Factory workers

Factories using iron machinery and steam engines sprung up all over the country, especially near the coal mines. New towns were built for the factory workers. The whole countryside changed.

By Victorian times people realised that the new industry brought new problems as well as new benefits. One of the biggest problems was the conditions in the factories.

What can you remember?

Fill in the gaps in these sentences with the right words from the following list:

blast furnace   coke   mines   manufacture

1   The invention of the _____ allowed iron to be made with

_____.

2   In 1837 children were allowed to work in _____.

3   With the industrial revolution most _____ took place in factories.

Something to do

1   Colour the pictures on pages 13 and 14.

2   Imagine you are a child working in a Victorian coal mine. Using writing and pictures, describe a day in your working life.

Workers

Population

Two changes were happening to the population of Victorian Britain:

1 It was changing from a **rural** population to an **urban** one.

2 It was growing enormously, as this table shows:

Year	Population of Britain (millions)
1801	10.5
1837	17.5
1851	20.8
1871	26.1
1901	37.0

Why?

Two reasons why the population rose so fast are:

1 Improvements in agriculture meant people were better fed and stronger.

2 Improvements in medicine meant that fewer people died young.

And so what happened?

More people meant more of everything else: more clothes, more shoes, more food, more pots and pans, more houses and so on. That meant more bricks, more factories, more ships, more towns and more jobs. And so the Victorians went on making and building.

So many children! The population of Victorian Britain went up and up

Conditions at work

The industrial revolution was something entirely new.

At first the government did not think it ought to get involved in what was going on. It left the workers and employers to sort things out for themselves.

But in time more and more people complained about what was happening:
- Women and very young children working long hours in terrible conditions
- Dangerous workplaces
- Low wages.

Reform

Gradually, the government brought in a number of **reforms** (improvements). Many of these were made by **Acts of Parliament**.

One of the first was the Mines Act, made in 1842. This said that women, boys and girls aged under 10, were not to work underground in mines!

That was not much, was it? Yet the Mines Act was a start. By 1901 there had been all sorts of other laws making work safer and better. Even so, children aged 12 could still be sent out to work.

A woman dragging coal in a mine

Trade Unions

Victorian workers wanted:

a   more pay
b   shorter hours of work
c   safer work places
d   help for workers who were sick, injured or unemployed.

To help get these things, they joined together in groups, called **trade unions**. To begin with, the law would not allow trade unions to do much. Slowly, however, the law was changed and trade unions became more powerful.

By the end of the Victorian period they:
1   could go on **strike** to get what they wanted
2   were setting up their own political party (it is now the Labour party) to help them in parliament
3   had done an enormous amount to make the lives of workers better.

What can you remember?

Read these sentences and put a tick (✔) in the box against the ones that are true:

1   In 1901 the population of Britain was 27 million.   ☐

2   The 1842 Mines Act said young children could work in coal mines.   ☐

3   An employer works for another person for wages.   ☐

4   Trade unions were set up to help workers.   ☐

Something to do

1   On a separate piece of paper, draw your own picture of the work going on in a Victorian factory in about 1840. Write about what you have drawn. You will find some more help on pages 4 and 13.

2   Say why you think the government did not want to get involved in what went on in mines and factories. _____

_____

_____

Towns

London

Look how the population of London grew: 1841 – 2 million; 1911 – 6.5 million.

For a long time it had been the biggest city in Britain. In Victorian times it became the biggest and most important city in the world.

It was an amazing place – huge, smoky and exciting. There were slums and palaces, museums and churches, shops and factories, houses and parks.

Other cities

Other towns grew as fast as London. In some ways this was even more surprising, because before the industrial revolution they had only been villages.

Many of these towns were in the north and midlands, near where the coal and iron was found.

Here are some of the towns which grew very quickly in Victorian times: Birmingham, Manchester, Liverpool, Glasgow, Sheffield, Newcastle, Leeds. Can you find them on a map?

Looking after the towns

The new towns and cities brought all kinds of problems, such as:
* keeping law and order
* getting rid of rubbish and sewage
* making sure the water was clean
* making roads and pavements
* setting up street lights
* seeing that houses were safe and well-built.

To do all these things the government made sure that each town had a council.

In time these councils were **elected** by some of the people living there.

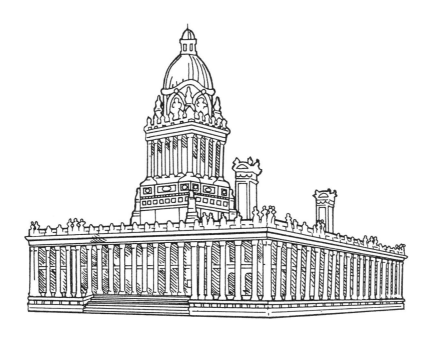

Leeds town hall, built in 1856 by the proud city council

What can you remember?

Put a circle round the correct answer:

1 The population (in millions) of London in 1911 was   9.6   6.5   5.6

2 Victorian towns were run by .   councils   the government   the working class

Transport and Trade

Getting about

Before the industrial revolution, the only ways of travelling on land were on foot, on horse (or donkey), or in a horse-drawn coach or cart. None of these were suitable for carrying very heavy loads.

In the 18th century canals were dug all over the country. A canal barge held much more than a cart. It could move as fast as the horse pulling it.

Railways

The biggest change in transport began in 1825, when George Stephenson opened the world's first public railway. It went from Stockton to Darlington. The trains were pulled by steam engines on wheels. At first they took only goods, but soon there were passenger trains as well.

In 1837 there were less than 1600 kilometres of railway track. By 1852 there were more than 9600 kilometres, and by the end of the century there were almost 31 000 kilometres!

Goods and passengers could now be taken all over the country quickly and cheaply.

One of the first passenger trains

Ships

Until Victorian times ships were made of wood. In the 1840s the first iron ships were built. One of the most famous was the *Great Britain*. It was built in 1845 by an engineer called Isambard Brunel.

Iron ships were stronger than wooden ones and could carry more. They were also heavier. They needed an engine. The answer was a steam engine, driving either paddle wheels or a **screw** (sometimes known as a propeller).

HMS Warrior, the first British warship made of iron

International trade

International trade goes two ways:
1 **Imports** are goods bought by one country from another
2 **Exports** are goods sold by one country to another.

Every country has imports and exports. Britain is a trading nation, always buying and selling things with other countries.

Victorian trade

Changes in transport made it easier for British goods to be imported and exported.

British manufactured goods could be taken quickly from the factories to the ports, then exported in steam ships.

At the same time, **raw materials** like cotton could be more easily brought to British factories. For a time Britain became the 'workshop of the world'.

Markets

British goods were sold all over the world. While Britain was the only industrial country, her factories made better, cheaper and more goods than anyone else.

But by the end of the 19th century, other countries – such as the USA, Germany and France – had also industrialised.

British businessmen had to compete with foreign businessmen and manufacturers. It was not so easy for them to win a market for their goods.

For example, the Germans were very good at making steel. They also invented the motor car. By 1900 Britain was no longer the most important manufacturing nation.

The British Empire

Many British goods were sold to the **British Empire**, a collection of countries which had Queen Victoria as their queen. Some, like India, were governed by the British. Others, like Australia, governed themselves.

They sent Britain most of their raw materials (tea, coffee, meat, iron, wood, cotton, etc), and bought British manufactured goods. This helped British industry.

The British Empire in about 1900 (shaded areas)

What can you remember?

Fill in the gaps in these sentences with the right words from the following list:

      exports   canals   invention   raw materials

1 The motor car was a German _____.

2 Britain brought in _____ from abroad, such as cotton and wood.

3 In the 18th century Britain was covered with a network of _____.

4 Britain's _____ were mostly manufactured goods.

Something to do

On a separate piece of paper, draw a picture of *either* a ship powered by paddle wheels, *or* an early railway train.

Disease

Health

One of the biggest changes between Victorian times and now is in people's health.

When Victoria became queen, doctors knew very little about what caused illnesses. They did not know much about making people better, either. They did not know, for example, that there were such things as germs. Operations could not be done without pain. There were not enough doctors or hospitals, and treatment was expensive.

Many babies died before they were a year old, and adults often did not reach the age of fifty.

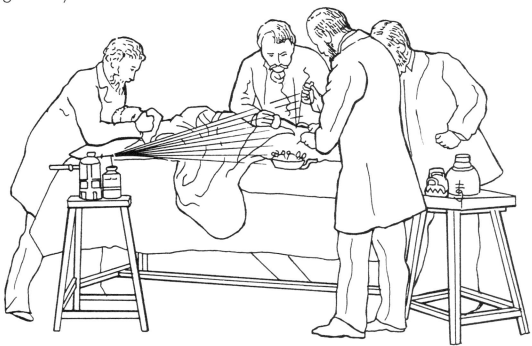

An early Victorian operation

Operations without pain

Before the 1840s operations had to be done as quickly as possible so that they did not hurt too much.

In 1842 an American doctor discovered that if patients breathed **ether** they became unconscious, and then difficult operations could be done on them without pain.

The trouble was that patients needed a lot of ether, and it exploded easily! Five years later a Scottish scientist found that **chloroform** was a better **anaesthetic** (substance which made people unconscious). Soon it was being used all over the world.

The world of bacteria

Although operations were painless, many patients still died of **infection**. The man who discovered germs (or bacteria) was a Frenchman named Louis Pasteur.

Louis Pasteur at work in his laboratory

Once bacteria had been discovered, there were two ways of fighting them:

1 Killing them. Joseph Lister discovered **antiseptics** (substances that kill bacteria). Thanks to his work, operations became safe and painless.

2 Inoculation. This was also discovered by Pasteur. It meant giving people a weak form of a disease, so they did not catch the real disease.

Nowadays babies are inoculated against all sorts of diseases, like diphtheria, that killed babies in Victorian times.

Problems

The wonderful work of Victorian scientists improved the health of the whole world. But it also produced problems.

As fewer people died young, the population of almost every country began to grow. And the population of the world is still growing incredibly fast. This leads to pollution, famine and poverty.

Chadwick's report – do something, or die

In the 1830s the government became worried. In the new towns there were terrible outbreaks of the disease **cholera** (a serious stomach infection). Not only the poor died, but people from the middle and upper classes as well.

The government asked Edwin Chadwick to organise an enquiry into what was going on. In 1848 Chadwick reported that the health of the nation, living in dirty towns, was awful. Unless something was done about living conditions, outbreaks of killer diseases like cholera would continue.

Public Health Acts

Chadwick's report said that the government should make sure drinking water was clean, build good lavatories and sewers, make sure dead bodies were properly buried and allow only pure food to be sold. But many people said they would rather risk getting cholera than be told what to do.

The first new health law (The Public Health Act of 1848) did not have much effect. Not until the 1870s did laws force people to start putting things right. Very slowly, the health of the nation began to improve. Cholera had been conquered.

What can you remember?

Put a tick (✔) in the box if the sentence is correct:

1 Ether allowed operations to be carried out painlessly. ☐

2 Louis Pasteur invented anaesthetics. ☐

3 The 1848 Public Health Act did a lot to help the health of the nation. ☐

4 Cholera killed only members of the lower classes. ☐

Something to do

Carefully study this picture of 1864 and answer the questions below.

Mary Evans Picture Library

1 Explain why you think the picture was called 'A court for King Cholera'.

_____

_____

2 Give the picture your own title. _____

3 This picture was drawn sixteen years after the 1848 Public Health Act. Why does it suggest that the Act did not do its job very well?

_____

Getting Children to School

Only the lucky ones

When Queen Victoria came to the throne:

- Anyone could set up a school and teach what they wanted in it.
- The government played almost no part in education.
- Children did not have to go to school.
- Most children went to school for 3 or 4 years at the most. They were taught about the Bible, reading, writing and arithmetic.
- Almost everyone had to pay to go to school.
- Only a few middle- and upper-class children stayed on at school after the age of eleven.

Poor children at the worst sort of Victorian school

Monitors

In many schools there were not enough grown-up teachers, so they only taught a few senior pupils. These pupils, called **monitors**, then taught the same lessons to groups of younger pupils. All this went on in the same room. Sometimes there were more than fifty pupils, all being taught in groups at the same time!

The punishments in Victorian schools were very strict – the most common was beating with a stick.

The work of the churches

Most schools were set up by religious groups. There were also church Sunday schools. Children who worked during the week could go to Sunday school to learn to read and write.

Church schools were usually well run, and they generally charged fees according to the parents' wealth. The very poor did not have to pay.

The government wakes up

In time the government began to play a part in education.

– why?

- The industrial revolution, with its complicated machines and paper work, meant that more educated workers were needed.

- **MPs** (members of parliament) wanted educated voters to choose the government.
- MPs thought that if people were educated, they would behave better, and not riot against the government!

– how?

- In 1833 the government gave a little money to some schools. The amount of money it gave slowly rose after this.
- 1870 – a really important year for education. Where there were no church schools, local people could organise a school board to set up their own school. Soon there were enough **elementary** schools for all pupils.
- Now there were enough schools, the pupils had to go to them. In 1880 the government said that all pupils had to attend school between the ages of five and ten. At ten they could begin part-time work in factories!
- In 1891 the government gave enough money for schools to stop charging fees.

A Victorian board school. Some school buildings like this are still being used – is there one near you?

Older pupils

By the end of the Victorian period most secondary school pupils still had to pay fees at a grammar or public school. Some grammar schools had **scholarships** for very able pupils.

As in 1837, normally only upper-class and middle-class children went to secondary school.

What can you remember?

1 Put a circle round the correct answer:

   a Board schools were begun in   1870   1860   1880

   b Pupils who taught other pupils were   MPs   fees   monitors

2 a Between what ages did pupils have to attend school in 1880?
     _____ and _____

   b Why did very few working-class children go to secondary school?

_____

Something to do

Using the pictures in this section, draw your own picture of a large Victorian schoolroom in which the teaching is being done by monitors. Colour your picture and label it.

Religion

A Christian country –

In Britain today there are many people of different religions – Christians, Muslims, Sikhs, Hindus, Jews and so on. In Victorian Britain nearly all religious people were Christian.

Religion was more important than it is today. Middle- and upper-class people talked about religion a lot and liked to be seen going to church. They often began the day with prayers, and thought of Britain as a Christian country.

Middle-class family prayers – can you see the servants?

– or was it?

But the working class were less sure about religion. They thought that religion was used by the other classes to keep the workers in their place.

Things were changing, too. For reasons which we will see below, many Victorians of all classes found it more and more difficult to keep their faith. By the end of the Victorian period, Britain was a much less religious country than it had been at the beginning.

The Church of England

In England and Wales the **Protestant** Church of England was the biggest and most powerful church. It had been set up by law, it was the church of the queen and parliament, and only its members (**Anglicans**) could do things like go to the universities of Oxford and Cambridge.

Gradually, however, the Anglicans gave way. By 1900 Roman Catholics and members of other Protestant churches did not feel quite so left out.

Nonconformists

Protestant Christians who did not belong to the Church of England were known as **nonconformists**. This means that they did not go along with the Anglican church. There were all sorts of nonconformist churches and groups. Most of them were very lively.

One of the largest and best known was the Methodists. Another group, begun in 1878 by William Booth, was the **Salvation Army**. The Army soon spread all over the world. It is famous for helping the poor and having fine brass bands.

William Booth

Religion and good works

Some Victorian reformers wanted to help others for religious reasons. The famous reforming prime minister, William Gladstone, was a very religious person. He believed that by helping others he was doing God's work.

The religious faith of other famous Victorians led them to help people less well-off than themselves. These included George Cadbury, the chocolate manufacturer, and Thomas Barnardo, who set up homes for children who had no parents.

Missionaries

Missionaries spread their Christian faith to people all over the world.

Many went to places where the Christian faith was not known, such as the centre of Africa. Very often they tried to help the people they met by teaching them to read and write and bringing them medicines.

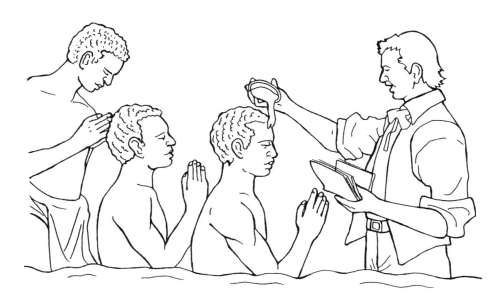

A missionary at work in Africa

What can you remember?

Fill in the gaps in these sentences with the right words from the following list:

Gladstone   Cadbury   Salvation Army   nonconformists

1   The _____ were Protestant Christians who did not belong to the Church of England.

2   George _____ was a manufacturer who tried to help the working class.

3   The _____ made a name for themselves by playing brass bands and helping the poor.

4   William _____ was a reforming prime minister.

Unbelief

The 1851 shock

On 30 March 1851 the Victorians carried out a **census** to see how many people went to church. The result was a real shock – only just over half the population went to church or chapel.

By the end of the century even fewer people were going to church or chapel – less than a quarter.

Why did it happen?

- New towns – when the new industrial towns grew up there were not always churches. So people got out of the habit of worship.
- The study of history – historians who studied the Bible closely found that it was not always historically correct. This led some people to lose their Christianity.
- Science – even more important was the work of scientists. Men such as Charles Darwin looked at how the world and everything in it began. Their work suggested that the Bible story of God creating the world in a week was not true. They announced:

  a   the world was much older than the Bible said

  b   human beings had not been suddenly made, but **evolved** from other creatures. This idea was known as evolution.

  None of this scientific discovery agreed with Bible stories, such as the one about Noah and the flood, and many people lost their faith.

The results

The decline in Christian religion upset many people. They thought that it would destroy British **society**. This did not happen. Instead it was easier for Britain to become a country of many religions, as it is today.

What can you remember?

What do these words mean?

Census _____

Society _____

Anglican _____

Something to do

Look carefully at this picture and answer the questions below:

A Victorian cartoon about evolution

1 Colour in the picture and say what the creature on the right is _____

2 For a long time almost all people thought God made the first man and woman – Adam and Eve. But Victorian scientists said that human beings had evolved from creatures like monkeys.

   How does this picture show that people found the new idea difficult to understand? _____

   _____

How do we know?

Sources

How do historians find out about religion in Victorian Britain? They find out from **sources**. A source is anything which tells us about the past.

Types of source

There are two types of historical source

1   **Primary (or original) sources** – These come from the time we want to know about. They are the best way of finding out about the past.

2   **Secondary sources** – These are usually books written by people who have studied primary sources. They are a quick and easy way of finding out about the past. Most of this book is a secondary source.

Something to do

Write in whether these are primary or secondary sources:

1   Queen Victoria's letters _____

2   A school history book _____

3   The drawing below, *based on* a Victorian cartoon _____

London, 1886. A meeting of people wanting reform

Primary sources

Four types of primary source are:

1 things written in the past, such as newspapers, letters, diaries or books

2 paintings, drawings, carvings, photographs and films

3 anything people made or built in the past – from railway stations to pots and pans

4 the spoken word, *either* recorded *or* said by people who were alive at the time.

Something to do

1 Sound recording was invented at the end of the Victorian period. Give two reasons why historians do not have much spoken **evidence** about the Victorian period.

   a _____

   b _____

2 In the space below, draw and label any piece of original evidence from the Victorian era. See if you can find something that has not been mentioned so far.

3 Here are two sources from the Victorian period, a picture and a piece of writing. They are from reports about children working in mines.

Derbyshire. In this district, the hours of work are commonly 14, and are sometimes extended to 16... , and the mines in general are most imperfectly drained and ventilated... .

Thomas Straw, aged seven, Ilkiston: They wouldn't let him sleep in the pit or stand still; he feels very tired when he comes out; gets his tea and goes to bed. John Hawkins, aged eight, Underwood: Is tired and glad to get home; never wants to play. Robert Blount, aged ten, Eastwood: He is always too tired to play, and is glad to go to bed; his back and legs ache; he had rather drive a plough or go to school than work in pit.

a   What sort of work did children do in mines? _____

_____

b   Why did Robert's legs and back ache? _____

c   Why did the children not want to play? _____

d   Why do you think employers liked children to work for them?

_____

Victorian Science

Another revolution?

The Victorian age produced many wonderful scientists. Their work changed the world and the way we understand it. These changes were so great that they could be called a revolution.

Medicine and living things

We have already noticed the main changes in the sciences of medicine and **biology**. We met the work of three famous scientists, Pasteur, Lister and Darwin. Can you remember what each one did?

Pasteur _____

Lister _____

Darwin _____

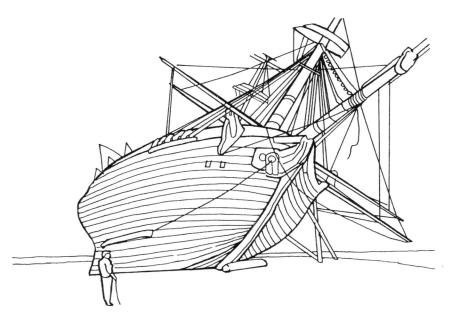

HMS Beagle being repaired during its voyage

Darwin spent years doing research before he came up with his idea of evolution. He got much evidence for his theory by making a long voyage in *HMS Beagle*, writing down what he saw and thought about.

There were other advances in this area of science, such as the discovery of X-rays and ways of treating diseases like **malaria**.

The two teles-

The two great Victorian communication inventions were the **telegraph** and the **telephone**. Television was invented later.

An early wireless telegraph

Telegraph

The telegraph was a way of sending messages down wires by using electricity. The first system was made in 1836. The messages were not speech, but bleeps. An American named Samuel Morse invented a code so that the bleeps could be understood. It is known as Morse code.

The bleeps are of two kinds:
- a long one, called a dash, written like this: —
- a short one, called a dot, written like this: •

The letters of the alphabet are made up of dots and dashes, for example:

A = • —   B = — • • •

It takes a lot of training to get the hang of the code!

Wireless

At the end of the Victorian period, Guglielmo Marconi discovered how to send messages through the air.

One of his first messages was in Morse code. He sent the letter S (● ● ●) across the Atlantic at 12.30 pm on 12 December 1901. His invention was called the **wireless telegraph**. Today this is known as radio.

Telephone

Alexander Bell, a Scotsman who went to live in the USA, discovered how to send the human voice down wires. He told the world about his telephone in 1879. Today there is still a Bell telephone company!

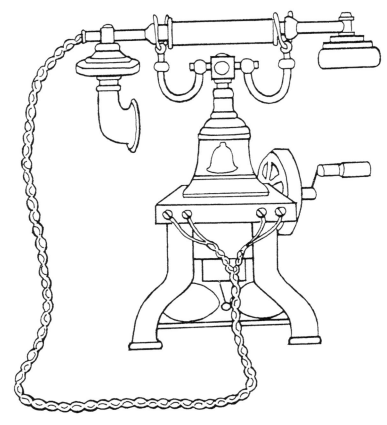

One of the first telephones

Electricity

One of the Victorians' most important inventions was how to **generate** electricity so that everyone could use it. It was first used in lighthouses.

The first light bulbs were made by Americans, Edison and Swan, in 1880. The first British power station opened two years later.

Cars, cameras, chemistry...

The list of Victorian inventions and scientific discoveries goes on and on. They:
- learned more about the enormous universe and tiny atoms
- made artificial cloth (rayon) and plastics
- invented petrol and diesel engines
- built **steam turbines** (a new kind of steam engine) for ships
- discovered photography, made the first cameras and took the first photographs.

What can you remember?

1   What was the name of the ship in which Darwin sailed? _____

2   Why was a wireless telegraph given that name? _____

_____

3   What is S in Morse code? _____

4   When was the first wireless message sent across the Atlantic? _____

5   What did Edison and Swan make? _____

Something to do

These pictures show a penny farthing bicycle of 1887 and a car of 1896.

a   Colour the pictures.

b   Label the differences between modern bicycles and cars and the Victorian ones in the pictures.

Great Builders

Bricks and steel

The Victorians built as no one had done before – railways, bridges, houses, colleges, factories, halls, markets and every other type of building.

Mostly they used the materials of the industrial revolution, bricks and steel.

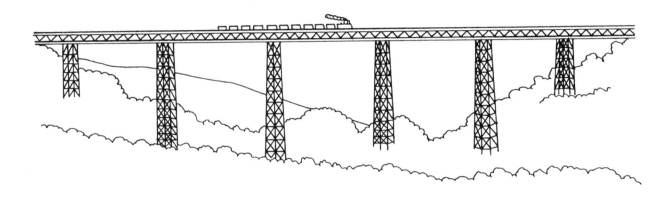

The Crumlin viaduct in Wales. When it was built in the 1850s, it was the largest bridge of this kind in the world

Styles from the past

The Victorians got many of the ideas for their buildings from history. There were two popular styles:
- **Gothic**, which was like the buildings of the middle ages (about 900 to about 1500), and
- **Classical**, which was like the buildings of ancient Greece and Rome.

Sometimes the two styles were mixed together in a real muddle!

The Crystal Palace

The Victorians put up one of the first modern buildings – the Crystal Palace.

This was a huge building of iron and glass. It was built in 1851 in the middle of London to house the **Great Exhibition**. The exhibition was a collection of the latest ideas from the industrial revolution. The Queen and all the British people who went to see it were very proud of what their country had achieved.

Art, Design and Photography

Photography

The first photograph was taken in 1826 – it took 8 hours to take!

Twenty years later the process had been speeded up quite a bit. It now took only 15 minutes to take a picture. But the equipment weighed almost 50 kg.

The first Kodak camera went on sale in 1888. Modern film had been made by the end of the century.

You may have seen an early camera, like the one below, in a film. It stood on a tripod and the photographer had to be covered with a black cloth to stop the light getting in.

A Victorian photographer at work

6 Science, Art and Leisure

Drawing

Nowadays we are used to seeing photographs of what is going on in the world. We see them on TV and in newspapers and magazines.

Before the invention of photography, drawing and painting were the only ways of making a picture of a scene. For example, we know what Crystal Palace looked like from drawings.

Crystal Palace, where the Great Exhibition of 1851 was held

What can you remember?

Fill in the gaps in these sentences with the right words from the following list:

> classical   Kodak   Crystal Palace   8 hours   15 minutes
> Great Exhibition

1 _____ buildings were based on the style of the ancient Greeks and Romans.

2 In 1888 the first _____ camera was made.

3 The _____ of 1851 was held in the large glass and iron building known as the _____

4 By about 1855 a picture could be taken in _____

Writers

Poets and novelists

Some of the best and most popular poems and novels were written in Victorian times. There were also many excellent children's writers, too. For example, Beatrix Potter's *Peter Rabbit* came out in 1900.

It was a great age for reading because:
* with the spread of education, more people could read than ever before
* there was no TV or radio, so reading was a popular pastime.

Charles Dickens

The most famous Victorian novelist is Charles Dickens. He was born in 1812 and died in 1870, so we say his **dates** were 1812–1870. This is sometimes written like this: 1812–70.

Almost certainly you have not read any of Dickens' books yet. But you may well know about one or two of them – they are often made into films, musicals and plays.

Have you heard of Scrooge, the miser from *A Christmas Carol*? Or some of the characters from *Oliver Twist* – perhaps Oliver himself, or Fagin, or Bill Sykes?

Charles Dickens

Sport and Leisure

Their own entertainment

The Victorians were used to making their own entertainment. They played a lot of indoor games, read books, told stories and had sing-songs round the piano – if they could afford one. Lighting by candles or lamps was expensive, so the poor did not stay up long after dark. For them the winter nights were long, cold and dreary.

Going out

There were plenty of things for the Victorians to do when they went out – as long as they had some money.

Fairs were common, so were horse races. Most towns had a theatre and a **music hall**. The theatres put on plays; the music hall audience was entertained with music, songs and jokes.

Drinking in pubs was popular with many of the working class. It gave them a chance to forget their hard lives. Towards the end of the period, religious groups like the Salvation Army tried to persuade people to drink less. Laws were made to stop pubs opening so often.

Victorians on Brighton beach, 1859

Something to do

As people got richer, so more and more began to take holidays by the sea. Colour the picture on the previous page. Label the things that are different from a holiday beach today.

Sports

Modern sports began with the Victorians. Of course, people have always played games. But the Victorians wrote down the rules and arranged proper matches in leagues and competitions. Cricket, football, rugby, tennis, boxing and golf were all organised by the Victorians.

The first Football Association cup was held in 1871 and the first cricket county championship in 1873. The Victorians also played the first international matches.

Women and sport

Towards the end of the Victorian period, women began to play more sport. Before this it was not thought proper for them to do more than gently ride a horse or take a walk. Now they started playing tennis and hockey, swimming and cycling.

They still had to wear clothes that got in the way, like the ones in the picture below. Can you imagine what it was like trying to play tennis in a dress like that?

Men and women playing tennis, 1886

What can you remember?

Put a tick (✔) in the box if the sentence is correct:

1 The dates of Charles Dickens were 1822–70. ☐

2 The Victorians organised the modern game of rugby. ☐

3 There was no TV in Victorian times. ☐

4 Towards the end of the 19th century women played more sport. ☐

Answers

Note: children may need help with the words in bold type.

Page 5: 1a = reigned, b = working class, 2 Upper, middle, working. Something to do = Great, great granddaughter. Page 10: 1 = population, 2 = aristocracy, gentry, 3 = manual work, 4 = running water. Page 11: 1 = 36 500, 2 = 901 – 1000, 3 = 20th. Page 12: 1 = 100 years, 2 = 19th, 3 = electric motors, petrol engines, 4 = pumping water. Page 14: 1 = blast furnace, coke, 2 = mines, 3 = manufacture. Page 17: 4. Page 19: 1 = 6.5, 2 = councils. Page 22: 1 = invention, 2 = raw materials, 3 = canals, 4 = exports. Page 25: 1. Page 29: 1a = 1870, b = monitors, 2a = 5, 10, b = could not afford it. Page 32: 1 = non-conformists, 2 = Cadbury, 3 = Salvation Army, 4 = Gladstone. Page 35: 1 = primary, 2 = secondary, 3 = secondary. Page 38: Pasteur = germs and inoculation, Lister = antiseptics, Darwin = evolution. Page 41: 1 = HMS Beagle, 2 = does not use wires, 3 = • • •, 4 = 12.30 pm on 12 December 1901, 5 = light bulbs. Page 44: 1 = classical, 2 = Kodak, 3 = Great Exhibition, Crystal Palace, 4 = 15 minutes. Page 48: 2, 3, 4.